BRITAIN IN OLD PHOTOGRAPHS

SHOREHAM-BY-SEA

PAST & PRESENT

EDWARD COLQUHOUN &

K.T. NETHERCOATE-BRYANT

Budding BOOKS

A Budding Book

This book was first published in 1997 by
Sutton Publishing Limited
Phoenix Mill · Thrupp · Stroud
Gloucestershire · GL5 2BU

This edition first published in 2001 by
Budding Books, an imprint of
Sutton Publishing Limited

Copyright © Edward Colquhoun &
K. T. Nethercoate-Bryant, 1997

Title page: Horace, a much-loved local
character, who carried on Shoreham's
entertainment tradition.

British Library Cataloguing in Publication Data
A catalogue record for this book is available from the
British Library.

ISBN 1 84015 213 3

Typeset in 10/12 Perpetua.
Typesetting and origination by
Sutton Publishing Limited.
Printed in Great Britain by
J.H. Haynes & Co. Ltd, Sparkford.

Report in local paper (20 August 1882): 'A Cricket Novelty – After a large amount of money spent on the improvements of the harbour of Shoreham, the inhabitants of Southwick and Shoreham were able to play a game of cricket on the Bar at the entrance of the Harbour, on Tuesday afternoon last. The sides were chosen by Mr Brazier of the Mistletoe Tug, and Mr Gardner of Southwick, the match ending after an exciting finish in a tie. Quoits were also played, and fireworks in honour of the event, were let off by a well-known resident of Shoreham. The match was witnessed by over one hundred persons.'

CONTENTS

The Dolphin features large in the history of Shoreham. Dolphin Chambers was an important building at the east end of the High Street. Harry Ricardo manufactured a motor car in the High Street called a Dolphin Car with a brass dolphin as a radiator mascot. It was not surprising then that H.G. Evershed, a soap manufacturer, used the name for his product.

INTRODUCTION

Henry Ford once said, 'History is Bunk!' Did he really mean that? Without a view of the past the same awful mistakes are repeated over and over again.

There is much more remaining of New Shoreham than of Old Shoreham, which lies to the north. Therefore we have concentrated on the past and present where it can be linked and compared in the 'old town' of New Shoreham. In our first book, *Around Old and New Shoreham*, we concentrated mainly on the two towns' peripheral aspects. This volume will spotlight some of the highways, byways, and alleyways of Shoreham-by-Sea as they are now, and as seen by the Victorian and Edwardian residents and visitors.

The layout of this volume was the brainchild of Mr Reg Leggett, a Shoreham resident and long time estate agent in the area. In 1957/58 Reg, with some friends, formed the Shoreham Preservation Society of which he became the first chairman. In 1964 he was instrumental in the emergence of the Historic Shoreham Preservation Trust, later to be renamed Historic Shoreham Trust. He was its chairman until his death, aged 90, on the last day of 1996.

Among the campaigns he led was the re-routing of the A27 flyover at the old toll bridge. It was originally intended to follow the line of the Upper Brighton Road adjacent to the Red Lion and St Nicholas' Church. Happily his efforts succeeded and the road/motorway now crosses the Adur further north. He was a friend and student of Henry Cheal, a local historian whose books, *The Story of Shoreham* and *The Ships and Mariners of Shoreham*, are still the most consulted books on the area.

This early suspension bridge was the first of three to carry the coast road over the River Adur. It was designed by W. Tierney Clarke, the architect of Hammersmith and Marlow Bridges. Much of the work was carried out by W. Ranger of Brighton. The suspension links were from a design by Cpt. Samuel Brown who was the builder of the Brighton 'Chain' Pier in 1823. The Norfolk bridge carried the arms of the Duke of Norfolk, a lion and a horse, on the suspension piers of the bridge. It was opened on 1 May 1833.

EARLY HISTORY

Shoreham existed as a settlement in the Neolithic period, and probably before that time when a land bridge connected us to the continent of Europe. In recorded history we know that Shoreham was established near the mouth of the river 'Score' or 'Sore'.

Selden, who was a Sussex man, says that at Shoreham Ferry (possibly the site of the Norfolk Bridge) the river was called the 'Weald Ditch'. The name Adur is fairly recent in the chronology of the county; it was first seen in *Polyalbion* by Michael Drayton, published in 1612. There is no firm evidence, as yet, that it was the 'Portus Adurni' of the Roman occupation period.

Shoreham as the nearest south coast port to London has always been an important entrepôt. From the late thirteenth century Shoreham exported large quantities of wool and salt from the surrounding countryside. The shipbuilding and fishing industries were also of great importance to the town. In the years 1323–9, fifty-eight recorded shipments of salt from Sussex ports to the continent were made. Only three shipments were recorded in the years 1395–9. It is believed that the 'Great Pestilence' (later known as the Black Death) was brought from the continent to this Sussex port in 1347/8, which may explain why the salt exports declined.

Improvements to the harbour in the eighteenth and nineteenth centuries and the laying of oyster beds within the river mouth brought prosperity to the fishermen and the carriers who made daily journeys to the capital.

An aerial view of the town and river, sometime after 1920. St Mary's Church can be seen on the north-east side of the old town. The footbridge is at the lower left of the picture and the railway bridge middle left. The old wooden toll bridge is above the railway bridge and the Norfolk Bridge is out of picture just below the railway bridge. The High Street can be clearly seen, skirting the southern part of the town.

ACKNOWLEDGEMENTS

The authors wish to express their thanks and appreciation to all those who helped with information and loaned prints and photographs which went to make up this publication, especially Darren Baker, Michael Baker, Warwick Baker, Mary Belton, Robert Campbell, Joan Dayer-Smith, Anthony Ellman-Brown, Zoë Ellman-Brown, Robert Hill, Reg Leggett, Peter Lucas, Chris and Jackie Martin, Michael Norman, Ted Norris, Trevor Povey, Jack Powell, Dick Powell, Leslie Stevens, Mrs J. Turner, Alan Upton.

Our thanks also to David Rudkin of the Marlipins Museum, David Tait of the Shoreham Society, Mr W.T.C. Barnett, Sen. Library Assistant, and Ms H.A. Stevenson, Group Librarian, of Shoreham Reference Library, Brighton Reference Library, and Adur District Council, who helped us with advice and material from their archives, for their goodwill for our project. Lastly our thanks to Mark Nelson, Anna and Andy Hylton of 'First Light' Brighton who prepared many of the old photographs for publication.

The authors would appreciate any corrections to the text, as with our last book we were able to revise the reprint with information supplied by our readers. Thank you.

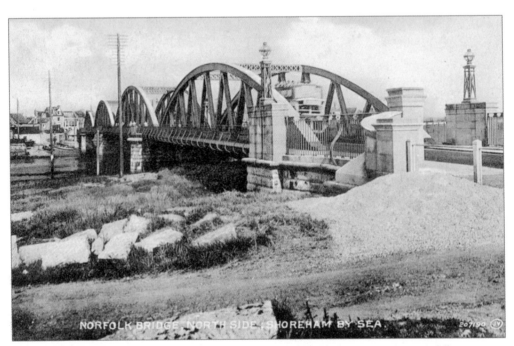

View of the four sections of the cantilever bridge. This structure replaced the ageing Norfolk suspension bridge (*see* Introduction). More functional but much less attractive than the one it replaced, the new bridge was opened by Lord Leconfield on 4 July 1923 and was still a toll bridge. Owing to the increasing motor traffic, and the congestion caused by impatient drivers, payments for crossing were abolished in 1927.

THE MAIN
THOROUGHFARES

The footbridge, from the north end. Known as the Dolphin footbridge it replaced the ferry boats which plied from Dolphin Hard to Shoreham Beach and Bungalow Town (see Section Four). This new bridge was constructed of reinforced concrete with a sliding centre section to allow for the passage of vessels upstream. It was opened on 3 February 1921 with appropriate ceremony by the Earl Winterton, MP for Horsham and Worthing. The toll was one penny. An old resident, Thomas Stow, was present at the opening. He had also been present at the opening of the first Norfolk Bridge eighty-eight years earlier.

High Street, east end. This narrow street is the main coast road to Southwick and Brighton. All of the buildings to the right of the road were demolished in the 1930s including Dolphin Chambers (centre); this was formerly the Dolphin Inn and is on the site of an even earlier Dolphin Inn. The lamp column (in line with the two posts) is a relic of a former classical building, *c.* 1711, which stood opposite Marlipins (*see* p. 13) and had ten such columns. The modern photograph, taken from opposite the entrance to Church Street, shows motor cars pulling out of East Street (left centre). A forest of masts sprout behind the Sussex Yacht Club, the only visible building on the south side of the road. Much shipbuilding took place along this part of the river; the slipways for large vessels were opposite East Street.

High Street, *c.* 1870 (east and looking east). This photograph must be earlier than the one opposite since the Albion Steam Brewery appears to be working here. Everything east of the Albion Brewery has been demolished, and since 1935 the area has been occupied by Coronation Green. The buildings to the right of the brewery chimney are much the same over 120 years later (minus two chimney pots). The building with the dormer windows was the post office.

The lower photograph shows the modern (1996) view. Beyond the unaltered buildings (right) can be seen the footbridge (*see* p. 7) and Coronation Green lies below the south pavement level. The penny toll for the use of the footbridge was abolished in 1938.

On the site of Coronation Green, some time in 1947, a boat auction is taking place. Small pleasure-boats were now being used by weekend visitors, many of whom rented bungalows on the other side of the footbridge. Fishing was a declining industry and hiring boats was another way to supplement the fishermen's income. Coronation Green is near the slipway where many of the larger vessels were constructed. Many small craft are now stored a little way to the east, in the Sussex Yacht Club.

The lower photograph shows the serenity of the garden several feet below the busy main High Street with seats for footsore and exhausted shoppers. An earlier picture of this area shows ferrymen awaiting trade; that there are some thirty men indicates that the ferrys were very busy at times. The East Street Arms on the corner of East Street was the watermen's local.

Brighton Road, looking north-west, after the Second World War. The houses in the top photograph were pulled down in the 1970s to make way for the new Civic Centre. They stood on land between Brighton Road and Ham Road to the west of St Aubyn's Street, near the Coliseum cinema which was also demolished. The Coliseum was originally built in the First World War (*c.* 1916) as a theatre to serve the thousands of soldiers billeted in Shoreham and on the hills behind (Slonk Hill). The Coliseum (right of top photograph) later became a cinema, no doubt showing films that were made in Shoreham as well as the latest from the emerging Hollywood film studios. The foundation stone of the new civic building was laid in 1979, and the completed red brick Adur District Council offices and centre were opened formally by the chairman of the Adur District Council, councillor S.R. Little, on 27 September 1980. St Aubyn's Street is on the extreme right in the lower photograph.

High Street, *c.* 1900 (looking west near junction with Middle Street). The coaching scene is a rerun of earlier regular coach journeys. The Dolphin Inn was the post inn but the Crown and Anchor (Tamplins Ales) was a coach stop and was also a gathering place for the local hunt to have their 'Stirrup Cup'. Note the turbanned figure on the west end of the inn; it was a ship's figurehead known as 'Tom Jones'. The Methodist church (right) was erected in 1879 and endured until 1936 when it was demolished along with many other old buildings.

In the lower photograph the turbanned figure has been replaced by the figure of a pirate/sailor which is said to have been carved out of a solid piece of teak some time in the 1930s. Standing on the bow of a boat he has kept guard over the High Street ever since.

Marlipins, High Street, 1880s (north side, corner of Middle Street). Now a maritime museum, Marlipins (with the chequered front) has been used for many purposes. It is probably the only surviving Norman non-ecclesiastical building from the medieval period in the town, dating from about 1100. Reconstructed in about 1300, it has had little alteration since. The deeds survive back to 1347 (the year the Black Death arrived) when it was described as an Oat Market. In the 1880s it was occupied by Messrs Gates. The Gates family is an old-established Shoreham family, resident in the town from medieval times; Major T.B. Gates was the last High Constable of New Shoreham. This snowstorm was evidently a memorable one; several other contemporary postcards depict its aftermath.

Apart from the refurbishment of the top windows there is not much visible difference in the building's outer appearance. However, the interior has been arranged to display artefacts and paintings to their best advantage.

High Street, looking west from the bottom of Church Street, after 1879. The top view shows what was part of the old market square. The area on the left of picture has been removed to widen the roadway. In the distance can be seen the buildings which in earlier times enclosed the market area. The photographs on pages 8 and 9 show the reverse view of other buildings on the south side of High Street sacrificed to the motor car.

The bottom photograph shows the new buildings on the south side. The Methodist church was demolished in 1936 to make way for the new layout. Up to the pirate figure on the Crown and Anchor the scene has not changed much in the hundred years since the first picture; the ornate gables (left) have been removed and replaced with plain boards but the end ridge tiles are still in place, and at pavement level there are still shops and offices.

High Street, looking south, 1870s. These old houses and shops are to the west of Ship Street Gap and were demolished in the 1930s to form the modern High Street. From the height of the chimneys it would appear that the original roof was thatched. Ship Street Gap gave access to the river for launching small boats and also to the shipyard which ran behind the row of shops to the Norfolk Bridge. The shipyard and slipway for large vessels were to the east end of the High Street, and the shipbuilding yard behind these old buildings was for smaller craft and also for fitting out ships launched from the east slipway. Part of the shipyard was owned by James Balley, the owner and builder of the Swiss Gardens. In this row was the 'shed' used by Harry Ricardo to fabricate his two-stroke Dolphin motor cars; later these premises were used for showing films and from 1909 was known as the Bijou.

High Street, north side, 1920s. The International Stores was earlier the International Tea Stores of 60 High Street and the 1914 directory names the manager as a Mr A.W. Parrott. The notice on the window announces that half a pound of Ceylindo Tea will be given to any customer spending half a crown. It appears that the store has seven assistants and a delivery boy; one wonders if the length of the fringe on the young men's aprons denotes their seniority? Inside the store the atmosphere would have been pervaded by the pungent aromas of freshly ground coffee, cheese, cured hams, and newly baked bread, smells that are not enjoyed today with modern packaging and marketing methods. Service was the watchword then – customers were served by an assistant from behind the counter. Butter was weighed and moulded into fancy shapes with wooden butter pats. There were bentwood chairs for the elderly and valued customer. The floor had fresh sawdust daily. Below, the modern-day view lacks the character of the top picture.

High Street, south side, west end, *c*. 1900. Burtonshaw's blacksmith shop was in the 'Old Shipyard' which was just off the High Street near the Bridge Hotel, as recorded in the 1902 street directory. The 1915 directory gives his address as 71 High Street and his residence as 8 Church Street. The 'Old Shipyard' area stretched from opposite Ship Street west to the Bridge Hotel. Presumably one had access to the river through the shop itself. The 1915 directory also mentions plumbing and kitchen fitting (see notice on door). It is likely that his main employment was as a ship-fitting blacksmith rather than as a farrier.

The lower view taken in the 1960s shows the above site after demolition and the notice board indicates that the land is for sale. The Bridge Hotel can be seen to the right of the telegraph pole, and the Ropetackle site is straight ahead. The King's Head is still standing; one can just see two of the three gables.

High Street, looking west, *c.* 1938. This is the south side of the west end of the High Street. The fish and chip shop was renowned for the quality of its food. Some 1930s nightclubbers made it their rendezvous, many of them arriving from outside the district. The shop was called 'Brighton Fish Stores' and at this time a portion of chips was one penny, with a generously sized piece of fish at tuppence. The top photograph shows the east side of the Bridge Hotel (right) which was demolished along with the shops and buildings in 1938. It was rebuilt in 1939 and set further back from the road. The lower photograph shows the rebuilt High Street, still dispensing fast foods.

High Street, looking north-east, *c*. 1909. This view shows the west end of the High Street from the Shoreham end of the Norfolk Bridge. There were iron gates at each end of the bridge, but they were removed in 1927 when the tolls ceased. One of these gates can be now seen at the entrance to Sele Priory at Upper Beeding where it is secured to two huge blocks of Sussex Winklestone. The gentleman collecting the toll from the motorist is probably Mr Burstow who is listed as toll collector in the directory of the time. The automobile is a Napier, owned by a resident of Bungalow Town. The horses are held by their drivers some way back from the emerging motor car, a wise precaution as these early vehicles could frighten the animals and cause them to bolt, which usually resulted in expensive damage to horse and cart, to say nothing of passers-by. The roofline in the High Street has changed little over the last ninety years, but the advertisements have been removed from the rooftops and the buildings have been tidied up.

High Street, west end, approaching Norfolk Bridge, *c.* 1880. The Bridge Hotel was built on the site of the earlier Fountain Inn. The building of the suspension bridge in 1833 brought more trade and a new hotel was built incorporating parts of the old Fountain, where there were regular entertainments in one of the large rooms. As well as accommodating travelling players and Freemasons' meetings, the room also did duty as a local courthouse. The great Victorian actor Hermann Vezin made his first appearance on stage here in the 1850s. Looking straight ahead one can see the toll booths and the first suspension tower of the bridge with the lion atop (part of the arms of the Duke of Norfolk). The modern view shows the flat concrete bridge which is the third to cross the Adur river at this point. The Bridge Hotel was demolished just before the Second World War and rebuilt further back from the road. The Fountain and the former Bridge Hotel were coaching inns used by the Arundel coaches up to the early years of the twentieth century.

West end of the High Street, opposite the Shoreham end of the Norfolk Suspension Bridge, 1880s. The top photograph draws our attention to the main occupation of the fishermen at this time, the oyster fishery. Next to the Fresh Oyster shop is a cooper's shop (lean-to building); oysters were transported to the capital and other cities on a regular basis. More than a hundred boats dredged oysters, some three times in two weeks from oyster beds in mid-channel. The oysters and scallops were sold to resident fish merchants who laid them in beds in the Adur river, known as oyster ponds, for later shipment. Henry Cheal (*Story of Shoreham*) records that 20,000 tons were sent by rail from Shoreham in one year in the 1850s. When steam vessels replaced the sailing dredgers the trade declined. The present-day photograph shows the empty site; this is where the earlier gas works stood with its landmark large gas-holder. The railway arches can be seen on the left.

The New Norfolk Cinema, Old Shoreham Road, looking from Victoria Terrace.

Old Shoreham Road, at the junction of Victoria Road, (looking south), 1930s. The New Norfolk cinema, built in 1935, is on the right of the picture, with the flagpole. Opposite is the garage and service station, formerly a blacksmith's, with hand-operated petrol pumps set back from the pavement. In the distance (centre) is the King's Head public house.

The modern picture shows the cinema demolished and Ballamy's SAAB showrooms on the site. There is now a clear view of the third Norfolk Bridge, since the houses and the King's Head Inn have been removed. The cleared area is known as the Ropetackle site and several ideas for its development have been put forward in the last few years, but at the time of writing no proposal has yet been accepted.

Victoria Road, looking north, 1920s. Victoria Road joins Southdown Road at its top end. Victoria Terrace named in the top photo is opposite the houses pictured. This name appears to have been discontinued from the 1920s since later directories do not record the Terrace separately. This view is the reverse of the picture on the opposite page. The iron bridge in the distance (left) carries the main south coast railway line to Portsmouth and the west and had a branch to Horsham (now defunct). The bridge was built in the 1840s when the Shoreham railway, opened May 1840, was extended to Worthing in 1845. In the gap (right) the car sales garage and forecourt replace Dodd & Sons cartbuilders of the earlier photograph. The newsagent's shop still thrives.

The old trestle bridge across the Adur, *c.* 1880. This very rare photograph is from the album of the Ellman-Brown family. This is not to be confused with the old Shoreham Toll Bridge, a similar structure to the north built in about 1781. The London, Brighton & South Coast Railway opened their Brighton–Shoreham line on 11 May 1840. There were six trains each way on weekdays, and it is recorded that on the second day of opening there were 1,750 passengers. Many of them visited the Swiss Gardens pleasure grounds; later in the 1840s as many as 5,000 persons were brought into the town in a single day. The extension of the railway line to Worthing was completed and opened on 24 November 1845, the wooden bridge having been constructed in 1844/45.

The old wooden structure was dismantled in 1896. The steel caissons of the new bridge are sunk some 70 ft into the river bed and filled with concrete. The steel bridge was designed by Sir John Aird.

Old Shoreham Road, looking north, 1880s. This scene is probably of the great snowstorm of the 1880s (*see* p. 13). Old Shoreham Road starts from the south at the High Street by the Norfolk Bridge and continues north to the old wooden toll bridge near St Nicholas' Church. At its junction with the Upper Brighton Road stands the famous Red Lion Inn. Parallel with the road ran the first part of the London, Brighton & South Coast Railway, later the Southern Railway. The lines ran along the east bank of the River Adur as far north as Beeding Cement Works where they crossed to the west bank and went on to Horsham. Beeding Cement Works straddles the boundary between Shoreham and Beeding and employed some 300 men at its peak production in the 1950s. Now with cheap imports of cement from former Iron Curtain countries, it has ceased to manufacture this commodity. Dr Beeching closed this line in the mid-1960s, but goods trains ran to the works until some twenty years ago.

East Street, looking south to the High Street and Dolphin Chambers, *c.* 1875. The top photograph shows the very narrow High Street and Dolphin Hard (extreme left). In the middle of the present High Street stood the Dolphin Chambers (last building left), built on the site of an earlier Dolphin Inn. The property was described as being in South Street in 1721 (M. Norman, *Walkabout Guide to Shoreham*) and having a slaughterhouse and a wharf on the south side. The Dolphin ceased to be an inn or public house in 1870. It was once owned by the Hannington family who later established the Hannington business in Brighton. The school building was described as a Church Sunday School in an early directory.

In the lower picture there is a clear view across the river where the Dolphin once stood. We are not sure if the school building is the same structure as depicted by the top view there are now five sash windows above the shopfronts of Sussex Stationers and the Imperial Cancer Research Fund shop. The Ferry Inn is on the south end of the row.

East Street, looking south-east, *c*. 1900. East Street, formerly Oriental Street and also known as Brewhouse Lane in earlier times, was the main road north and the way to the railway station from the High Street and the ferry (later footbridge) from Bungalow Town and the beach. The entrance to New Road is at the extreme left of the photographs and 2 and 4 New Road were built in the back garden of the seventeenth-century house with the decorated front. M. Norman (*Walkabout Guide to Shoreham*) relates the pedigree: owned by George Wilson in 1782, in 1815 it passed into the hands of the Hide family where it remained until 1903. From the Shoreham directories, and from census material, it would appear that East Street was always a commercial area – almost every trade has been represented here.

Apart from the ubiquitous television aerials the rooflines do not appear to have changed much since the first photograph was taken but shop fronts have been added to all the buildings.

East Street, looking north, early 1900s. The Foden steam wagon involved in this accident has a Brighton registration number and may have been delivering sacks of barley or malt for brewing as there was a brewhouse recorded in East Street. The accident appears to have happened outside the Otter public house. As most inns had cellars it is possible that the weight of the wagon was too great for the roof of the cellar and it ended up with its nearside wheel below the road level. Alternatively the wagon could have been delivering to Paris at 18 East Street. Steam wagons and traction engines with solid wheels had been the cause of complaint for many years as the vibrations caused by their passing brought down old flint walls and buildings. The modern photograph shows the war memorial and beyond to St Mary's House in the distance and the other part of East Street beyond New Road (right).

East Street, looking north from a point west of New Road, *c.* 1910. Sunday School treats and school outings were regular events before the Second World War when a large percentage of schoolchildren attended Sunday School. Many of the outings were to Bramber where the castle grounds contained boatswings and other amusements, teashops abounded and boats were for hire on the Adur river. There was also the great attraction of Potter's museum of curios and stuffed animals arranged in cases; the Death of Cock Robin, the Kittens' Tea Party, and the Guinea Pigs' Cricket Match were all admired by the children. The wagons in the photograph are owned by a Mr Wood, but driven by the Bowyer brothers who had stables in John Street.

The bottom picture shows the War Memorial against the churchyard wall and the recent no-entry sign (1996). St Mary's House in North Street can be seen through the trees in this winter photograph.

St Mary's churchyard, 1870s. The earlier photograph shows East Street, on the extreme left. The photograph is from the Ellman-Brown family album and the caption in the album is 'Old House, Churchyard . . . (late J. Elbs) Mrs Hindless the tenant standing at the door (pulled down)?' The houses on the south side of the churchyard wall may have been part of St Saviour's College, believed to have been founded by that great educationalist, Nathaniel Woodard. Woodard was curate from 1847 and the college lasted until the 1870s. He went on to found Lancing, Hurstpierpoint and Ardingly educational establishments.

   The lower photograph shows the north wall of the National Westminster Bank. The brick arch (extreme right) is still visible, but the burial vault (centre) has been lowered with the top slab now at ground level. Some gravestones are still upright about 120 years on.

St Mary's, early 1900s. The Old Vicarage (in North Street, top of East Street looking to the north) is an eighteenth-century house with a notable portico and oak staircase (M. Norman, *Walkabout Guide*). Nathaniel Woodard, founder of Lancing College, was the curate to William Wheeler, the vicar of Shoreham (Old and New). Woodard attended to the needs of the folk of New Shoreham and lived at St Mary's House. He started a day school there in January 1847 with twenty-four pupils and two masters, the forerunner of the Lancing College we know today. Legend has it that the pupils lived mainly on bread and cheese and 'Milestone Pudding', so far apart were the currants, alleged the pupils, that there was a mile between each one! Captain Henry Roberts lived here in the 1780s (*see* p. 52). He was in charge of the long boat when Cook was killed on Hawaii.

Apart from the removal of some of the trees, the lower photograph is not very different from the earlier one.

Brunswick Road, looking south, *c.* 1907. Brunswick Road is a continuation of East Street, going north. The east end of North Street forms a dog-leg between East Street and Brunswick Road giving access to the railway station from the High Street and footbridge area. Tarmount Lane leads east from the far end, as seen in the picture. The entrance to Western Road can be seen on the right of the photograph.

The lower picture shows little change except for the removal of the attractive gas lamp. Lloyds Bank now occupies the walled area on the south corner of Western Road along with the main post office. There appears to be little change in the width of the road although the pavement now affords more room for the bank and post office customers.

Brunswick Road, looking north, 1940s. This is the reverse view of the one opposite. The railway level crossing, west of the station, can be seen in the distance. On the other side of the crossing is Buckingham Road, in earlier times known as Buckingham Lane, which gives access to the Upper Shoreham Road (the A27). Brunswick Road is one of three main shopping areas in the old town, the others being High Street and East Street. The photographs were taken from points at the west end of Tarmount Lane. In the top picture (lower left) you can see the east end of St Mary's Road, which is a continuation east of North Street. Western Road can clearly be seen in the lower photograph, left, distinguished by the shadows of late evening. On the right of the top picture are the Wesleyan church and hall, both built in 1900. The Methodists record that they were built in seven months with the first services being held in the summer of 1900.

Brunswick Road (postcard date stamped/post cancelled, 17 April 1905). Ham Road is on the right. Shoreham railway station is behind the Burrell Arms. The tram rails run to Hove via Portslade and Southwick. The tramway was first opened in the 1880s when the carriages were drawn by steam engines. Originally, it extended to the Swiss Gardens, but later the terminus was as pictured at the Burrell Arms. Some time around the turn of the century the cars were powered by horses and the full journey took over two hours to complete. At the beginning of the First World War the trams ceased to operate and the rails were taken up during the war.

The same view today shows the automatic barriers which replaced the heavy crossing gates. The signal box is no longer there and the semaphore signal gantry has been removed. The decorative work on the south wall of the Burrell Arms has been added since the first view.

Brunswick Road, looking north-west, *c.* 1900. A similar view to that opposite, this photograph shows the west side of the road approaching the crossing. Ham Road is on the right of the photograph. The Burrell Arms is on the right and the Buckingham Arms public house is on the left where the horse and cart are parked. Both public houses were built to serve the railway passengers of the new (1840) line. The locomotive on the crossing is probably a Billington 2–2–2, several of which worked the South Coast Line in the late Victorian period. The level crossing is built on a rise; when the railway was extended westward in the 1840s the line gradient had to be increased to cross the Adur river. The railway bridge had to be high enough to allow vessels upstream to serve the cement works at Beeding.

Shoreham railway station, looking west, *c.* 1870. The top photograph shows the station with the platforms lit by gas lamps. The earlier station building is much lower than the modern one because it was built before the line was raised for the Brighton to Worthing and Chichester lines in the mid-1840s (*see* p. 35). Beyond the station is the Buckingham Arms (centre). The semaphore signal gantry is not shown in the 1870 photograph but no doubt the pole west of the level crossing was some sort of signalling device. The lower picture shows Watning House built on the north side of the Buckingham Arms. This house is now used by the mental health authority. The shelter over the platform has been lengthened and extended and the old heavy crossing gates have been removed and replaced with automatic barriers.

Buckingham Road looking north, showing the aftermath of the great snowstorm of 17 January 1881. Known as Buckingham Lane up to 1900, and as Camp Lane or Camp Road during the First World War, it was the main thoroughfare between the town and the encampment on the Downs at Slonk Hill which housed the soldiers of Kitchener's Army. The Buckingham family took their name from the Manor of Buckingham. John de Buckingham signed a deed in 1220 relating to the Priory of Sele at Beeding, and the name has, with different spellings, passed down the years. The local telephone directory lists a score or so of Buckinghams. The top photograph reveals that there are no houses on the east side of the road as far as can be seen above the bank of snow. How well the old gas lamps look compared with the modern electric lamps in the 1995 picture. Buckingham Road is now one of the main residential areas between Old and New Shoreham. It runs from the railway station to the Upper Shoreham Road (A27).

Buckingham Road, looking west, 1880. At the south end of Buckingham Road, this house is named Buckingham Lodge and was the residence of John Ellman-Brown, who can be seen in the top photograph with his children. John Ellman-Brown was a local worthy and connected with John Ellman of Glynde. An enthusiastic archaeologist, he took great interest in the history of the town. By profession he was a ship broker, as was his father who was High Constable of Shoreham at one time, and had offices on Church Street. He was vice-consul to five nations, and for many years held the office of Clerk to the Local Governing Body, a position later held by his son Mr Harold Brown; between them they served almost fifty years. His interests extended to the Shoreham Regatta and he was the first Honorary Secretary of that annual fixture, first held in 1854. The modern photograph shows that the Lodge no longer stands alone.

Buckingham Road, looking north, 1920s. The triangle is at the north end of Buckingham Road. Both arms of the road join the Upper Shoreham Road. The memorial seat to the fallen in the First World War is clearly visible in the top photograph. The 1995 photograph shows some thinning of the trees which are now more mature. Shoreham was noted for its elm trees, which were planted in every road and lane and punctuated every hedgerow. Mr Norman says that they were obviously planted by the lord of the manor as part of a considered plan to provide timber for shipbuilding and domestic needs. They were an attractive and noteworthy feature. It is recorded by some local historians that many of the elms were used during the Napoleonic wars to provide gunstocks for the army. Apart from the road signs and markings the area has not changed very much over the years.

Buckingham Lodge, looking west, 1890s. The view in the top photograph is of the old first lodge to Buckingham House (*see* p. 74) on the Upper Shoreham Road which runs from the old wooden toll bridge across the River Adur to the east of Old Shoreham. Buckingham House was rebuilt in 1782 and the lodge may have been built at that time. In the days of the horse and carriage the lodge keeper was expected to be available day and night to open the gates to the landowner and his respectable visitors while turning away any undesirable riff-raff. The lower photograph shows the modern view, with the entrance to the Triangle leading to Buckingham Road on the left side of the picture; the rebuilt lodge is the house on the extreme right. Most of the houses were built in the 1920s and '30s by Gates, the local builders.

Buckingham Lodge, looking north, *c*. 1911. The new lodge was built on the site of the earlier one. There are two gates, one for carriages and motor vehicles, and one for cyclists and pedestrians, both open; no doubt they were closed at night against casual callers. In the 1914 directory the occupant of Lodge Gate was one William Russell. The road leading to Buckingham House appears to have many well-tended flower beds. At the end of the First World War Mr W.G. Little bought the main house, which had been empty for some years, and built a large house nearby. It may have been at this time that the new lodge house was built. Buckingham Park was acquired by the Shoreham people in the 1920s and is very well used for most sports and shows, with intermittent use by travelling circuses and funfairs. The lower photograph shows the lodge in its present-day setting. The road to Buckingham House is now built on and access is via The Drive.

Slonk Villa, later Slonk View House, 1890s. This house stood on the corner of what is now Eastern Avenue and the Upper Shoreham Road (formerly the Upper Brighton Road). Eastern Avenue forms the boundary between Old Shoreham and Kingston parishes. Slonk Hill is the high ground to the north of the parish which is now crossed by the modern Brighton bypass. In the days that the house was built there was a clear view of the hill but all the twentieth-century building has now obscured it. The villa was still standing at the time of the First World War and is recorded on a map of 1917. On this site today is a public house, the Green Jacket. During the Second World War a flying bomb narrowly missed the Green Jacket to explode in the allotment gardens in Eastern Avenue. The gardens had been used in the past by William Oliver, a nurseryman, resident at Slonk View House.

MINOR ROADS & SIDESTREETS

*The Little Wonder in John Street before 1907, when
it was shut down along with other less salubrious inns
and public houses which had caused much
drunkenness in the town. The people standing outside
the pub could include Mr A. and Mrs Baily who are
listed as the occupants in the 1903 directory.*

Victoria Road, looking south, 1897. This photograph shows part of Victoria Road from the railway bridge to the entrance to Hebe Road at its west end. Victoria Road was named in honour of Queen Victoria so it seems appropriate that the celebration of her golden jubilee should take place in her namesake street. The flag in the top photograph appears to be the 'Red Duster', the red ensign of the Merchant Navy which is at the head of the deep sea fishermen and crews of the cargo ships from Shoreham. Many children are taking part, possibly from schools and Sunday schools. The parade was making for Buckingham Park where many of these occasions terminated. Perhaps the marquee on the right was for further celebrations of Queen Victoria's 'golden' year. The lower photograph demonstrates the changes since 1897.

Victoria Road, looking north, *c.* 1912. At its north end Victoria Road merged with Southdown Road at the junction with Mill Lane. The ivy or creepers on the house on the left have been removed by 1995 and the house has gained double glazing. The knifegrinder's machine in the middle of the road would not survive long in today's traffic, but in 1912 one could see a horse and cart a long way off. The knifegrinder was a frequent visitor to residential areas, sharpening almost everything with an edge, scythes, axes, and all manner of cutlery. The knifegrinder's barrow, usually made from bicycle parts, had pedals for its motive power. The operator was often an ex-service man from the Boer War or later the First World War.

West Street, looking north, *c.* 1880. West Street runs from the High Street to the railway line – the
bridge can be seen in the distance. Contrast the top view of the wide road, as yet unmade, with the lower
photograph, the road made up and further restricted by the parking of the ubiquitous cars. The old flint-
walled store on the left has been used as a sailmaker's loft, and also used from time to time as a
contractor's store and carpentry and joiner's workshop. It is believed that the men with the ladder were
employed by C. Curd, a local builder. On the right-hand side of both upper and lower views can be seen
the West Street Primitive Methodist Church, erected in about 1860. Now redundant, the church building
serves as a boys' club. At the turn of the century it was used by the Salvation Army who later moved to
New Road.

West Street, looking north, *c*. 1920. A generation on from the photograph at the top of the opposite page, West Street has not changed much. The photographs record the terrace of houses in the area known as Sugden Place. This small area south of the railway line was at one time unofficially called White Lion Street, after the public house of that name on the west side of West Street. Before the construction of the railway in the 1840s West Street ran uninterrupted from the High Street to join Victoria Road at its north end. From early times West Street had been called Ropewalk or alternatively Ropemaker's Lane over its entire length because of its role in the ropemaking trade which was vital to shipbuilding operations in the town. The part of West Street to the north of the railway line is still known as Ropewalk.

Ship Street, looking north, *c.* 1959. Ship Street runs from the High Street to North Street incorporating Cavendish Place. M. Norman (*Walkabout Guide to Shoreham*) says that what survives of Shoreham's character is now to be found in the sidestreets. The building across the top of the road is the old Beehive Inn, which along with many other public houses was closed down in a town purge of drunkenness in 1907. The Schooner Inn at the other end of Ship Street was not considered a problem at that time and survived the 1907 'thinning out'. The lower picture reveals a much refurbished Beehive building. The waste ground is now a much-needed car park in this part of Shoreham. White Lion Court must have taken its name from the public house in Ship Street.

John Street, looking north, *c.* 1900. John Street runs from High Street north to the railway. It follows a curve as do the other side streets to the west of Middle Street. The name was originally St John's Street. This is a relic of the Knights of St John, the Hospitallers, who took over much of the Knights Templar properties when that order was suppressed by King Edward II in the early fourteenth century. It is known that the Templars held land in Sussex, in the Shoreham area, as well as Shipley, Sompting, Saddlescoombe and Southwick. The children in the top photograph are outside the public house the Little Wonder (*see* p. 43) which was closed down in 1907. Nearby is the Providence Baptist Chapel. Almost every sidestreet in Shoreham had an ecclesiastical presence of one denomination or another. The lower scene does not show any major change, although the gas lamp has disappeared – what a pity they could not have been adapted for electricity.

Middle Street, looking west, c. 1915. The crowd is outside 7–10 Middle Street. We do not know what the gathering was for but it looks like an outing of some sort. There is a soldier in uniform and presumably the coach drivers are in white coats and peaked caps sitting at the front. We do know that the man with the child sitting front row, extreme right, is Frank William Bowles, or Balls, recorded in the directory of 1914. He lived at No. 11 and had five daughters born in 1908, 1911, 1914, 1916, and 1920. The Burtonshaw family had one of their smithies with forge opposite this view. They were well-known blacksmiths and had several businesses in Shoreham, established in about 1830. Charles Burtonshaw, the last blacksmith in the old town, died in 1981. The lower photograph shows a more useful edifice but not nearly so mellow. There is a car park to the rear of the toilets.

Church Street, looking north, c. 1900. This is the east side of Church Street, which runs from the High Street to the north-west corner of the churchyard of St Mary (de Haura). Church Street was in earlier times known as Star Lane, Star Street, Church Lane and Rotten Row. Michael Norman (*Walkabout Guide to Shoreham*) says that the Star Inn on the south-east corner of Church Street was modernized in about 1900, but he thinks that it was a medieval building from evidence in the old cellars beneath the present building. The inn had a very noticeable sign that hung high above the High Street on a beam supported by uprights. In the late eighteenth century the Star received some six coaches a day; it was described as the 'best in the town' if somewhat poor. Meetings of the Christian Society took place in the Star. The members of this society had been deprived of their votes by Parliament in 1771 for corruptly conspiring to sell them; perhaps 'Rotten Row' goes with 'Rotten Borough'. The lower photograph shows the modern shop (1996). Although little has physically changed in the last hundred years, long gone are the days when one could buy a dozen bottles of beer for 2s 6d.

Church Street, *c.* 1905. At this time 18 Church Street was the office of John Ellman Brown, a ship broker. (He was the father of John Ellman-Brown, one-time High Constable of Shoreham.) The house was built in 1754 with four bedrooms. It was the former home of Captain Henry Roberts who twice circumnavigated the world with Captain Cook. He was later the master of a King's Revenue cutter. The seamen lining the pavement are thought to be the survivors of the *Liburna*, a sailing ship which was wrecked off Shoreham, 15 March 1905. It is not known for sure if the captain of *Liburna* is in the photograph; Commander Howard also served with Captain Cook on some of his voyages.

The lower picture shows very little change to the outside of the building, the most significant visible alteration being to the glazing bars on the windows.

Church Street, looking north to the churchyard wall and trees of St Mary's Church, 1910. The occasion pictured in the top photograph was on the day of the funeral of King Edward VII; Edward was buried in St George's Chapel, Windsor and nine kings attended his funeral. Parades were held in every town and village. The people in uniform are probably the local militia, but on these state occasions the police and fire brigades turned out with the scouts and boys' brigades. It was to be another four years before the Great War started. The sergeant on the right of the parade is most likely wearing medals from the Boer War. In the middle distance, right, can be seen the arch of the Star Lane Chapel, later to become the Star Picture Theatre, The Star Electric Picture Palace, and Winton's Hall. The bottom photograph (1995) shows little basic change in eighty-five years.

Pond Road, looking west, *c.* 1900. Pond Road is a continuation of both Middle Street and Church Street at their north ends. Pond Road is crossed at its north end by Western Road. The photograph shows the headmaster's house (left) and part of the Shoreham Grammar School buildings on the corner of North Street. It is recorded that there was once a large pond in this area. The headmaster's house is pictured in the prospectus of 1880 standing alone on the south-west corner of Pond Road. Both pictures here show the extra floor, which extended the house considerably. This must have been completed before the 1880 picture on the prospectus, which shows it with an extra storey but without the bay windows.

Shoreham Protestant Grammar School, Pond Road, 1960s. The grammar school was first established in New Shoreham in 1842. The founder was Mr W.H. Harper, although it is not known for sure that he served as headmaster. The prospectus for 1880 states that the principal was Mr Geo. F. Denman. It also says that 'At this establishment young gentlemen are liberally boarded and carefully educated'; Latin and French were included in the usual subjects at 30 guineas per annum, with an extra 4 guineas for drawing, piano and dancing. With his clothes every pupil was expected to provide his own knife, fork, spoon and towels. In 1965 the school vacated the premises and moved to Worthing. A few years later the school returned to Shoreham, acquiring a property in St Julian's Lane and using St Julian's Church as the school chapel. In the early 1970s the buildings in the top photograph were demolished and a new community centre was built and opened in 1974. The lower picture shows new buildings; the community centre is set back from the road and is obscured by the trees.

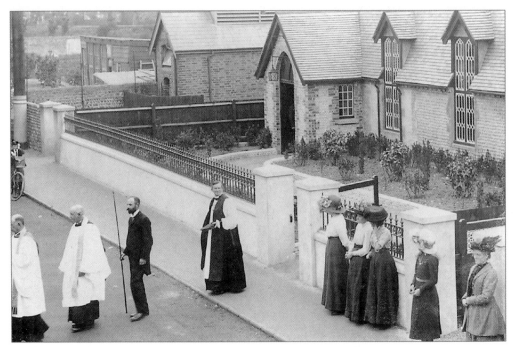

Pond Road, looking north-east, *c.* 1900. Above is Shoreham Grammar School chapel, but the occasion involving the clergy is not known to us. The chapel had been, at one time, part of the almshouses to the north of St Mary's Church. Beyond the chapel building is the old playing field/playground of the school. It is thought that this area was the location of the 'pond' in Pond Road. The land behind the chapel was variously known as Calverhouse Croft, Almshouse Field and also as Burrscroft; the latter name has been used for the nursing home which can be seen in the lower photograph behind the steps. The steps lead to the new Shoreham public library and reference library, the staff of which have been very helpful to the authors. This building was opened by Mr Clifford Musgrave (a well-known Brighton historian) in June 1969.

East Street and New Road, looking east. New Road can be seen straight ahead. The occasion shown on the postcard is the opening of the Church Hall and Sunday School by the Bishop of Chichester, 19 July 1912. The photograph was taken from where the war memorial was to be erected after the First World War. The houses on the right are described by Michael Norman as much older than the ones on the north side. The south side was inhabited mostly by ship's captains and owners. The south-side houses were built on a low cliff that formed the old river bank and are one storey higher at the back. In the lower picture is the well-known ironmongers, Curd's. It appears that the Curd family are long-time residents in Shoreham if the directories are anything to go by. They had a carpentry business in the 1914 entry, in Rosslyn Road.

New Road, *c.* 1900. East Street can be seen crossing the entrance to New Road behind the horse-drawn carts. The east end of the street joins the main coast road near the south end of Surry Street. The shop on the right was a butcher's and poulterer's owned by Walter Harry (Tom) Avis. Walter retired in the 1920s and took up smallholding at Mill Hill. In his spare time he became a Special Constable, rising to the rank of an Inspector in the Special Constabulary. He was also a governor of Old Shoreham Church of England School. He was well known locally for his generosity to the poor of the town throughout his business life. It is not known whether he appears in the photograph.

The lower picture shows the decline of this busy scene – the tiled front and decorative windows are all that is left of a once thriving business.

New Road, looking east, *c.* 1880. This is the junction where New Road meets Tarmount Lane. Tarmount Lane was an old lane leading from Brunswick Road to the shipbuilding area. Tarmount may indicate that tar was used in this area, probably for caulking the ships' planking with oakham and melted pitch. On the left of the top photograph is the early Wesleyan Methodist Chapel, built in 1829. This building replaced the Methodist chapel in Star Lane (now Church Street) which had been built in 1800. In 1900 a new Wesleyan church was built in Brunswick Road and the New Road Chapel was sold or rented to the Salvation Army. The old chapel can be seen in the lower photograph as two flats with one garage. It was converted in 1921 and is now No. 27 New Road. The old police station was in Tarmount; the 1903 directory lists A.G. Charman, Sergeant of Police and two police officers.

New Road and Tarmount Lane, looking west, *c.* 1900. New Road is on the left with Tarmount Lane taking the right fork; this is the reverse view of the photographs on page 59. The 1829 Wesleyan chapel is second from the right in the top picture. Fryar's House (double bay) is next to the chapel, now Friar's Court. This was owned by the Gates family. In the nineteenth century the Gates were one of the largest shipowners in Shoreham. When their fortunes declined in the early years of the twentieth century the Gates sold Friar's Court to the soap manufacturer W.G. Evershed. The house in the centre of the picture was called Athol House and was built by the Gates for the owner of the Derby winner 'Blair Athol'. In the 1903 directory it is occupied by Major T.B. Gates and in 1914 Frederick Thorowgood is in residence. Athol House was pulled down in the 1970s and replaced with a block of flats, Swanborough Court.

Surry Street, looking north, 1945. Surry, or Surrey Street (both spellings have been used in the past) stretches north–south between Ham Road to the north and the coast road, Brighton Road to the south near the junction with New Road. The top photograph reflects the joy at the cessation of hostilities in Europe with the unconditional surrender of Germany, 8 May 1945. The street party was to celebrate this occasion; almost every street in Britain had a party on this day with rationed foods being carefully hoarded in the last weeks of the war. Many of the children present in the photograph will no doubt be in their sixties now and the picture will remind them of the end of the 'dark days' of the second great war of the twentieth century. The houses in the top photograph have now been demolished. It is a shame that these old and mellow cottages could not have been refurbished for the next generation.

Surry Street, looking south, *c.* 1960. The reverse view of page 61 with open waste ground on the south side of the street. A few years later the houses on the right were pulled down and flats were built on the site. According to the Shoreham & Southwick History Workshop in their transcribed census returns of 1881, Surrey Street was a narrow lane with a cul-de-sac of little dwellings called Paradise Cottages. It was one of the most crowded of Shoreham's streets; in the 32 occupied cottages lived 171 persons, an average of 5 persons per dwelling. Seamen were the largest group here: 14 mariners were listed in the census, along with 8 general labourers, 7 agricultural workers and 2 blacksmiths. At the far end of the street on the left is the back wall of the Surry Arms. The Austin Princess looks out of place, but indicates the approximate date of the photograph. Below are the flats now on the site of the earlier picture.

Surry Arms, *c.* 1963. Surry Arms public house is, despite its name, in New Road, on the south-east corner of Surry Street facing the river. This area was known as Friar's Croft, and at one time was owned by the Carmelite friars of Shoreham founded by Sir John de Mowbray early in the fourteenth century. It is probable that this land also once belonged to the Templars. The Carmelites were said to have been inundated by the sea in the latter part of the 1400s. In 1492 they took over Sele Priory at Beeding, which had been a Benedictine house since the Conquest but had failed in 1458. This area was built on at the beginning of the nineteenth century and was for the working population, the exception being the south side of New Road which was older and housed many of the ships' masters and owners. The area north of New Road contained most of the town's lodging houses in the later nineteenth century (*VCH*, Vol. VI).

New Road, looking north, 1950s. Nos 61–75 were pulled down in the 1960s; flats now occupy the site. Pashley Court can be seen in the lower photograph. The flats were named after Cecil Pashley, a Shoreham aviator from the early days of flying at Shoreham Aerodrome. The Pashley brothers established a flying school at Shoreham airfield when it was little more than a saltmarsh. Eric left in 1916 to join the Royal Flying Corps and accounted for ten German aeroplanes before he was himself killed in action in France. His brother Cecil became a civilian instructor at the Grahame-White flying school, and taught generations of pilots, RAF and civil, at Shoreham. He died 10 December 1969. Tiger Moths draped with black ribbons overflew his funeral as a tribute to this popular airman.

Southdown Road, looking west, 1900s. Southdown Road runs north from Buckingham Place to the top end of Victoria Road and the junction with Mill Lane and was called New Barns Lane before it was built up. At the south end stood Longcroft, a large house and garden with many glasshouses, the home of the builder James Britton Balley, shipbuilder and first owner of the Swiss Gardens. Balley was the builder of many fine ships and credited with constructing the biggest vessel launched from Shoreham, the 800-ton *Blair Athol*, described as the largest barque ever built by Messrs Balley. Sadly Balley died before the ship was launched. Edward Goodchild (landlord of the Buckingham Arms) bought the Swiss Gardens from Balley in 1852 for £17,000. Goodchild lived in Oxford Villa, Southdown Road. The lower view reveals that the iron railings on the front walls have been removed; they went to help the war effort as scrap early in the Second World War.

Southdown Road, looking north, *c*. 1880. The top photograph is by W. Page, a well-known local photographer who lived at 35 East Street. The picture is from the collection of the late John Ellman-Brown who sold the cottages in 1891. The cottages form three dwellings and the lower photograph shows them still in place although much altered and refurbished. The tall chimney has been removed and three dormer windows have been added to the original structure. The photographs are taken from the north end of Victoria Road at its junction with Southdown Road looking towards Mill Lane. The 'kissing gate' (centre, above) leads to the Upper Shoreham Road via a footpath. Mill Lane also leads to the Upper Shoreham Road in a curve and goes on to cross the hill to the farm at Erringham.

Southdown Road, looking north-west, January 1881. The top photograph is of the three cottages again, showing the direction of Mill Lane which runs from Buckingham Road to the Upper Shoreham Road, and continues as Erringham Road on to Mill Hill and Erringham Farm. There was a windmill on Mill Hill but it is more probable that it was named after the windmill at the top end of what was to become Queen's Place, since the road served both mills. The five-bar gate on the left is the entrance to the burial ground to the north of the Swiss Gardens situated behind the houses on the west side of Victoria Road. The snow fell on the night of 17 January 1881; William Page, a local photographer, took a series of pictures around Shoreham which have been drawn on heavily for dating various scenes. Below, the view today.

Mill Lane, looking west, 1881. This photograph was taken from the top of Southdown Avenue by the three cottages on pp. 66–7. Mill Lane forms part of the parish boundary, which (says Henry Cheal) is always the sure sign of antiquity in a highway. Cheal suggests that the mill that gave its name to the lane may have been a water-mill as he has traced three water-mills in the medieval period. His researches confirm that one was in New Shoreham and two in Old Shoreham, probably in the area of Little Buckingham Farm where one building showed signs of housing a waterwheel. Water-mills were the first type of grinding mill; windmills did not appear in this country until after the Norman Conquest. The earliest recorded windmill was in the mid-twelfth century. There were or have been two windmills on the top of Mill Hill; one was burnt down and the other disappeared at the turn of the century. In the lower photograph Oxen Avenue is on the right and the entrance to the burial ground is on the left.

The Kissing Gate, 1900. This is probably the entrance to an ancient trackway which was a continuation from west of the town passing up Victoria and Southdown Roads. It leads to the Upper Shoreham Road, running parallel with the modern Oxen Avenue. The 'Kissing Gate' is a gate that allows the pedestrian to pass through but prevents large animals, horses and cattle from entering. Old custom says that if boy meets girl at the gate the boy can prevent the girl from passing until he is given a kiss. In this age of equality the boy would probably get a 'righthander'. The elm trees in the top photograph can be compared with the earlier picture opposite which shows that some years have elapsed between the two photographs. Looking at the modern photograph (1995) one wonders if the tree on the lane entrance is a relic of the top picture.

The entrance to the cemetery in Mill Lane, 1930s. The cemetery was established in 1886 when the churchyard at St Mary's was running out of space. The top photograph shows the lychgate and lodge probably built when the rest of Mill Lane was built up; before there was just a five-bar gate. The lychgate (corpse-gate; 'lich' means a corpse) was a roofed gateway where the pall-bearers rested if necessary, and usually there was a place to put the coffin off the ground. With the modern funeral arrangements (motor hearses and the like) the lychgate became redundant and the lower photograph shows that it has been removed at some time since the Second World War. There has also been an extension to the lodge.

VETERANS' RACE · SHOREHAM SPORTS 1907

Near Queen's Place, 1907. The windmill is located to the west of Queen's Place, and Mill Lane. A map of the parish dated 1873 indicates that the windmill was for milling flour. The map shows open space to the north of the windmill so much building has taken place in the thirty odd years after the map was produced. A mill was recorded on this site in 1724 but this would not be the one in the photograph as it was a post mill and the one in both pictures is a tower mill, i.e. a mill built of masonry with only the top cap able to rotate to face the wind. This mill was dismantled some time between 1907 and 1920 as Henry Cheal in his *Story of Shoreham* (1921) states that it had been dismantled. The lower picture shows workmen demolishing the mill. Old residents believe that Gates' men are pictured atop the mill. The mill field was used for sports, as can be seen in the top photograph.

Queen's Place, looking south, *c.* 1904. Queen's Place runs from Buckingham Road to Mill Lane. The postcard, postmarked 1904, is a view of the road toward the railway embankment to the south. The west side is built up but the east side of the road is only built up halfway; the rest is open ground with houses in Buckingham Road backing on to this space. The Shoreham & Southwick History Workshop comments on the 1881 census: 'Queen's Place had a middle-class air, its residents were typically master tradesmen, master mariners, professional people such as tax collectors and retired persons.' The children in the photograph appear to be well dressed in the Edwardian style. The modern photograph shows the scene basically unchanged as far as the buildings are concerned. The motor car has taken over the street preventing children's games of marbles or whip-and-top which could be played here up to the Second World War in reasonable safety.

North Street, corner of West Street and Sugden Place, *c.* 1882. The top photograph is from the albums of the Ellman-Brown family. The caption in the album is 'New House and Old House, bottom of Rope Walk (late Coleman's) both pulled down. Roman Catholic school built on the site' (that was demolished in 1903). Before the railway divided the road, West Street was part of the road known as the Ropewalk, which stretched from the High Street north to the junction of Victoria Road at its north end. Rope was manufactured here for the shipbuilders of Shoreham. The height of the chimneys in the top picture indicates that the cottages were thatched in earlier times; a thatched roof needed high chimneys to carry the sparks away from the thatch. The bulks of timber in the yard point to the fact that the occupants were probably builders or connected with the shipfitting business. Perhaps the square hole in the flint wall was for rope making. West Street can be seen on the extreme left in both pictures, and to the right the corner of the west end of the Beehive public house is just visible.

Buckingham House in Buckingham Park, *c*. 1900. By a deed dated 11 July 1657, Edward Blaker, described as of Old Shoreham, Gentleman, left to his wife Dorothy, should she outlive him, 'The manor house called Buckingham House' which he had newly erected, with the dovehouses, barns, stables, gaterooms, courts and appurtenances. He also named Newfield, Eastfield, Tenne Acres, and Southfield, all of which were part of a farm called Buckingham Farm. Edward Blaker had rebuilt the manor house on the site of an older house, also called Buckingham. Dorothy was the daughter of Henry Goring. Edward's brother William, Sheriff of Sussex in 1684, eventually inherited the house. He died in 1703 and the house passed to his grandson, William Monk. It was sold to Colville Bridger in 1766 and remained in his family for several generations. Buckingham House was subsequently owned by Henry Head, who was generally well liked because of his interest in the inhabitants of Shoreham. He died in 1905 and the property was left empty for some years before being purchased by W.G. Little who built a new mansion nearby (H. Cheal).

Longcroft, *c.* 1900. Longcroft was built by James Britton Balley on a large plot at the corner of Hebe Road and Southdown Road. Balley was the entrepreneur who established the Swiss Gardens. He was also a shipbuilder of some note. Edwards & Balley's shipyard built around four large sailing vessels each year and did much repair work for London ship owners. On James Balley's death Edward Goodchild took over Longcroft and the Swiss Gardens and made many improvements. It was at one time a girls' school, and during the Second World War a unit of the Canadian Army occupied the premises.

Longcroft was demolished in the early 1970s to make way for the blocks of flats seen below – what a change from the earlier elegant building.

Raven Road, looking north, *c.* 1885. Ravencroft House can be seen centre right in the top photograph. Note the open fields on the right-hand side. It was around here that soldiers were encamped in the Napoleonic wars. Henry Cheal says, 'Our registers of one hundred years ago betray the presence of the West Essex Militia, 5th and 44th Regiment of Foot, 10th Battery of Artillery, 10th Dragoons and Marines.' Soldiers were also billeted here in the early years of the First World War.

The present view shows that blocks of flats now occupy the area of open fields known in the nineteenth century as Buckingham Gardens.

FUNERAL OF PRIVATE HAROLD BERNARD STANDEN
OF C.Co. C™ CYCLIST BATTALION ROYAL SUSSEX REGT.
AT SHOREHAM-BY-SEA FEB 2ND 1915

Western Road, looking east, 1915. Western Road stretches from Brunswick Road to John Street. The top end of Pond Road can be seen on the right at the end of the wall. On the left is the road passing under the railway arch leading to Buckingham Place, which gives access to Southdown Road and the cemetery in Mill Lane. The high wall topped with the poles and netting borders the playground of Shoreham Grammar School in Pond Road. The photograph supplies us with an accurate date, and the occasion is the funeral of Private Harold Standen, late of the Royal Sussex Regiment (Cyclist Battalion). We do not know if he was a casualty of the war or whether he was the victim of a cycling accident. The grammar school buildings in the top picture are long gone and the Shoreham Community Centre now occupies the site. Burrscroft nursing home is on the other corner of Pond Road.

Shoreham Camp, *c.* 1914. In September 1914 the first of thousands of young soldiers, known as Kitchener's Boys, arrived at Shoreham railway station to be marched up Buckingham Road to a camp consisting of several bell tents. Their stores and provisions had sadly gone astray, and to add to their misery it was pouring with rain. Many were given food and shelter by generous residents who took pity on them. The top photograph calls the assembly 'The Camp in the Valley', probably in the area below Slonk Hill now occupied by Greenways Crescent and New Barn Road. The stand of elm trees in the distance could be in Hammy Lane. The bell tents look very white and probably unused – a good target for the Zeppelins! The lower photograph shows the top of Downsway.

Slonk Hill Camp, 1914. Mill Hill is on the skyline on the left. In the winter of 1914/15 many of the soldiers were billeted upon the inhabitants of an area that stretched from Brighton to Worthing. This was a temporary measure until more permanent shelter could be found. Then followed the building of the hutments, during which time the camp was pitched in Buckingham Park and the Oxen Field, which became a tented plain (Cheal). Older residents remember battalions of men marching along the High Street and over the Norfolk Bridge to take their morning and afternoon 'dip'. They would sing lustily 'It's a long way to Tipperary' and 'Who's your lady friend' along with other songs of the time. Later, rows of wooden huts covered Buckingham Park and New Barn Road.

Shoreham Camp, Slonk Hill, 1915. The soldiers returned from their civilian billets along the coast and were drilled and trained as fighting soldiers, now joined by the Canadians and other overseas volunteers. This first contingent was thought ready for the war in France and formed the Army's 24th Division, leaving Shoreham for the Western Front in June 1915. Further enlargements to the camp were made up until the end of the war in November 1918. By this time there were large YMCA recreational buildings and a special gymnasium in the east camp in the Buckingham Park area. There was a time of suspense when the news filtered through to the local population from survivors that the 24th Division had been terribly 'cut up'. King George V and Queen Mary visited the camp on two occasions during the war, in November 1916 and again in March 1918.

SWISS GARDENS

The Swiss Gardens were one of Shoreham's main entertainments attraction. Established in 1838 by James Britton Balley, the shipbuilder, the pleasure grounds were thought to rival Ireland's Pleasure Grounds on the Level at Brighton. The ballroom (150 × 54 ft) was the finest on the south coast with a refreshment area for upward of 1,000 persons. Among the pastimes were bowls, archery, theatre, a magic cave, an ornamental lake for boating, and a tall tower from which to observe the surrounding countryside. The school in Victoria Road is now on the site of the old ballroom. Balley died at Longcroft in 1863 and the gardens passed through several hands. There is still a public house on the site.

Swiss Gardens, east entrance, c. 1900. This entrance lodge is very similar in design to the western entrance lodge in the Old Shoreham Road. It was situated in the Victoria Road north of the railway bridge and opposite the Hebe Tavern on the corner of Hebe Road and Victoria Road. This was most likely the busiest entrance as it is the nearest to the railway station. The notice-board states that admission was a shilling, a fairly large sum in those days as many shopworkers and those 'in service' were only paid half yearly, and then for many it was perhaps a guinea per annum. Their clothing and accommodation were part of their wages, so they did not see much cash in their pockets.

The lower photograph shows the road known as Swiss Gardens which joins the Upper Shoreham Road at Connaught Avenue (north end). The school is to the right of the picture. The crossing warden is Mr B. McIntyre, premises manager of the school.

Swiss Cottage, Old Shoreham Road, 1920s. In the 1909 directory it is listed as 'The Cottage Inn, rear of the Swiss Gardens, Walter Eldridge proprietor'. The towered lodge in the top picture was removed in 1980. The public house has been added to on its north side and much of the area is now the pub car park. The chimneys on the main roof are unaltered.

The former 'New Ballroom' of the Swiss Gardens, 1880s. It was said, probably correctly, that this was the finest ballroom on the south coast. It was 150 ft in length and 54 ft wide. Designed by Arthur Loader (architect) it had two round towers, one at each end, and four smaller cupolas along its north side. The view in the top photograph is probably in the late 1880s or even 1890s as the roof is no longer in place. This could be for repairs, but more likely signals the dismantling of the building. The present-day view below shows the school playground of the Victoria Road School; the school occupies much of the Victoria Road site that was the western end of the Gardens.

Swiss Gardens Theatre, *c.* 1913. The theatre was demolished in 1913 along with the east entrance lodge in Victoria Road (*see* p. 82). The Gardens closed early in the twentieth century; as Henry Cheal remarked, 'the pleasures of one generation were not the pleasures of the next'. As its popularity declined it became in time the favourite 'haunt' of a somewhat rough element of the town, and it was then considered 'not quite correct' to go there. However, after the Gardens closed there were occasionally performances by local amateur theatrical groups such as those given by the Adur Minstrels and other concert parties.

The lower photograph shows the modern road called Swiss Gardens. The theatre site was probably somewhere in the middle distance and part of the present roadway.

The Glasshouse, 1890s. The Glasshouse stood on the corner of Old Shoreham Road and Freehold Street on the western corner of the Swiss Gardens site. The Swiss Gardens were originally that, a well laid-out series of gardens with an assembly room. The ballroom, theatre and other attractions were laid out in later years as it became more popular with visitors. A master gardener, James Evans was resident in Commercial Terrace in Old Shoreham Road between Buckingham Street and the west lodge. We have no dimensions for the Glasshouse, but compared with the seat (right) it must have been about 40 ft high, and some 50 to 60 ft in diameter, a huge structure for those times. The chimney indicates that it was heated, perhaps to rear exotic shrubs and plants which were a feature of the Gardens. The lower photograph is of the Swiss Cottage car park on the site of the former greenhouse which collapsed in 1915.

The Swiss Gardens, *c.* 1930. There were two boating lakes, West Lake and East Lake. They were probably fed by an ancient stream, the Northbourne, which drained surface water from the higher ground around Old Shoreham. The top view is of the rustic bridge which crossed the bottleneck between the two lakes. At this time the Swiss Gardens had been shut for many years, but Fred Pigott kept the Swiss Cottage pub going, utilizing the lakes and other amenities that still existed in the area behind. The lower picture shows an enamelled sign, a relic of the latter part of the life of the Gardens. Now entrance was free, but no doubt one had to pay for the separate services that were formerly covered by the admission charged by Balley and Goodchild. The fact that it flourished for more than seventy years was testimony to the good management of a series of owners. A similar attraction on the Level at Brighton, Ireland's Pleasure Grounds, failed after only four years of operation in 1828.

Buckingham Street, looking west, *c.* 1949. Buckingham Street is a cul-de-sac off Old Shoreham Road on the east side. On the other side of the wall at the end of the road is East Lake of the Swiss Gardens, one of two lakes there for boating and resident wildfowl. James Balley, builder and owner of the Gardens, built Buckingham Street to house his artisans and other low-paid employees. Many of these were musicians in his orchestra that played daily for all events and dances. There were more than thirty dwellings in this small street built in the 1840s.

The lower picture shows the blocks of flats that replaced these humble dwellings. That the hoardings are still in the same position today is a testimony to the advertisers who first used the site to inform the southbound traffic of available goods and services.

BUNGALOW TOWN

*A view of Old Fort Road, 1920s. The harbour is at
the top of the photograph with one of the naval giants
that later became the Nab tower at Portsmouth. The
Church of the Good Shepherd can be seen at the fork
in the road at the bottom of the picture.*

What was known as 'Bungalow Town' was built on a spit of land formed by the eastward drift of shingle through the English Channel. From about the tenth century the mouth of the River Adur has slowly been pushed towards Hove. In 1651 Charles II made his escape there from Cromwell's men after the battle of Worcester. The outlet of the Adur was then near the site of the present-day Hove Lagoon.

Although there were dwellings on the beach in the 1880s, and probably long before, it was not known as Bungalow Town until early in the twentieth century. Neb Wolters (1985) credits Marie Loftus, a music hall star, with building the first of the structures of the conurbation, Bungalow Town. Initially it was a colony of people from the entertainment world, principally the stars of the music hall and stage. As it developed it also attracted many outside the theatre, providing holiday and weekend retreats for the well-to-do. Local entrepreneurs erected chalets for rent to these people, a large proportion of whom had an entry in *Who's Who*.

Early in the twentieth century films were shot on the beach. Studios were erected here because of the splendid light on this coast which was vital for good filming with early cine-cameras. This growing industry drew in more entertainers, cameramen, and all the support 'behind the scenes' workers.

A great many of the dwellings were, basically, redundant railway carriages. The London Brighton & South Coast Railway had established a carriage works in 1913 at a site now covered by the Churchill Industrial Estate at Lancing. Without the wheels and bogies these carriages, placed together with space between, and roofed with corrugated iron or asbestos, made instant chalets.

Services, water, gas, electricity and proper drainage, were sadly lacking before the 1920s and many residents had water delivered at 2d per bucket. They used oil lamps for lighting and solid fuel stoves for cooking.

There were many ornate designs of railway carriage homes to be seen. Some survive to this day, a testimonial to the shipwrights and boatbuilders that made up the workforce in those days. The Second World War brought to an end the little village on the beach when the army requisitioned the land to fortify it against invasion.

A railway carriage being delivered across the Adur river on a vehicle normally used for transporting large trees and timber. St Mary's Church can be seen above the buildings in the centre.

The 'Mystery Towers' were built by the Royal Engineers early in 1918 near the entrance to the harbour. Constructed of concrete and steel with watertight compartments which could be flooded, they were intended to be two of a series which could be sunk in the English Channel between Dover and France. They could have anti-submarine nets suspended between them and be equipped with hydrophones to detect enemy vessels. At the end of the First World War one was towed to Portsmouth and sunk to become the Nab tower off the Isle of Wight.

Shoreham Beach, c. 1910. Many of the early seaplane trials were held on Shoreham's coastal area. Pictured above is Piffard's seaplane with a British 8 cylinder ENV motor; the propeller was said to be some 10 ft long. H.H. Piffard was the first user of what is now the oldest licensed airport in the country. Many experiments on early flying machines were carried out at Shoreham Aerodrome. King's Cup air races were a feature of the 1930s.

Beach Green Parade, 1930s. The parade was on the corner of King's Drive and the main Brighton–Lancing coast road. Adur Garages can be seen on the extreme right of the top photograph. King's Drive ran north from Beach Road across the main road to the railway halt, Bungalow Town station. There were two main sources of milk for the Beach area: Fred Batten and Chater's Dairy. Fred used the ford near the footbridge site with his horse-drawn float and Chater worked from the dairy pictured above. Mr Chater retired to Upper Beeding where he passed away a few years ago in his eighties. He related the tale to us of the onset of the Second World War. In 1939 the army evacuated the beach of residents who had 48 hours to leave the area. He was unable to collect that week's milk money and had a hard time as a result. The Royal Coach public house, built in 1957/8, can be seen in the lower photograph.

Old Fort Road, looking east, 1930s. This is the junction of Old Fort Road with Shingle Road. Shingle Road went from Old Fort Road north toward the river and joined with Riverside Road on the south bank of the Adur. In the top photograph telephone poles are being erected along the road. Telephones were luxury items in the pre-war days and only the very well off or businesses had one. From the number of insulators on the cross pieces of the poles it would seem that everyone had an individual wire to the exchange! The number of private telephones on the Beach must reflect the number of music hall, stage and film actors/actresses who had to be in close contact with their agents for work. The tall building on the left was called The Bungalow in 1915 but by 1930 had changed to Holidays. Hetty King, the famous male impersonator of 'All the Nice Girls Love a Sailor' fame, lived there and was often host to another well-known music hall star, Vesta Tilly. By 1996 (below) the scene has undergone some changes.

Tit-Willow, Mascot, St.Vincent, Woodcot, The Cabin.

Beach Road, looking west, *c.* 1923. This is the south side of Beach Road opposite the Weald Dyke. In about 1930 many of the bungalows were given numbers for Post Office reference. The Cabin was 94, Woodcot West 96, Woodcot 98, St Vincent 100, Mascot 102, Tit-Willow 104, but with changes of owners came changes of name and Tit-Willow later became Sedgmoor. Woodcot and St Vincent were owned by Miss Loy Smith who owned several others on the Beach; perhaps she was one of the entrepreneurs who had got into the holiday letting business as did many of the music hall people. This above view shows dwellings with upper storeys which cannot strictly be called bungalows. Several had a small lean-to annexe to house outdoor gear, bicycles and often the toilet. With no running water in the early years it was necessary that they had plenty of ventilation. The lower modern view shows well-appointed houses with gardens and garages.

Old Fort Road, 1920s. The Leggett brothers and friend on their motorcycles. These belt-driven machines would only reach 50 miles an hour in those days but the 'young bloods' used the roadway as a racing track, much to the dismay of the residents. Perhaps the fact that some motor racing stars like Sir Malcolm Campbell lived on the beach at times may have influenced their quest for speed. Fred Batten the milkman often pushstarted Campbell's Bugatti in the mornings; starter motors were not usually fitted to cars like the Bugatti and the starting handle was a permanent fixture. The bottom photograph is of a group of scouts who presumably met on the beach. The photograph was probably taken in 1910, and the scout master may be wearing medals from the Boer War. Perhaps he was with Baden-Powell in that conflict. The brother of N.E.B. Wolters (Bungalow Town Theatre & Film Co.) is in this group of scouts.

Beach Road, *c.* 1913. Etheldene was No. 38, near the King's Walk end of Beach Road and opposite the Mardyke. At this time it was owned or occupied by F.E. Sendall. Few, if any, of the bungalows and houses built on the beach itself, that is the south side of King's Walk, Beach Road, or Old Fort Road, have survived. When these light, prefabricated (railway carriage) buildings were erected a concrete slab, known as a 'raft', was laid several inches thick. Upon this foundation were placed two redundant railway coaches minus the wheeled bogies, allowing space in the area between them as required for the living room. The coaches became the bedrooms. The whole was roofed over and with matchboard ceiling and walls for the rest, you had the finished dwelling. Unfortunately, nobody had allowed for high tides which coincided with winter gales. A series of storms undermined the pebbles on which the concrete rafts rested. These then collapsed into the sea and the rest slowly followed.

Old Fort Road, 1920s. The bungalow is 176 Old Fort Road, named Desiree and owned by a Miss Heale (in the 1915 directory). There were many tennis courts around the beach. There was a tennis club in Ferry Road, 'Arthur's Club'; perhaps this party is connected in some way. Apart from sea bathing tennis appears to have been the main recreational pursuit for the people of the film colony and many competitions ensued on the beach. The lower photograph reflects the style of living in these lightly built structures. There was a piano in most living rooms with an organ as an alternative. The walls and ceiling were matchboard. In the centre is a cast-iron stove with the chimney passing through the ceiling and out through the asbestos or corrugated iron roof. These places were firetraps and many were burned to the ground when they caught fire. The fire brigade was stationed across the other side of the river and the fire engine had to traverse the Norfolk Bridge to get to Bungalow Town.

St Monica's School, East Meadway, possibly during the First World War. East Meadway runs east to west between Ferry Road and Shingle Road inland of Old Fort Road. One of the problems facing the early settlers on the Beach, if they were parents of school age children, was education. Before the footbridge was built in 1921 one had to cross by ferry or get to the town by the main coast road and the Norfolk Bridge, a lengthy trip. Mrs Baker, in a large bungalow called La Marguerite at the east end of Beach Road, ran a small private school where many of the younger Beach dwellers started their education. In the early days of the 'island' this was the only school on the Beach. The older children went by ferry to the Shoreham Grammar School in Pond Road, or to the convent in Southdown Road, New Shoreham. Others went further along the coast. St Monica's School opened a little later than Mrs Baker. Shoreham Beach First School is now established in Shingle Road.

MIGNON COLLEGE VIEW CLAREMONT THE VIEW

Lower Beach Road, looking south-east, *c*. 1915. There was some realignment of roads before and after the Second World War. These bungalows in the top photograph are listed in the directory for 1915 and again in 1930 as being in Lower Road and Lower Beach Road respectively. Mignon was owned by Mrs Elphic, College View was occupied by Mrs Brewster (presumably the college in College View, is Lancing College on the other side of the airport). Claremont was owned by Mrs A.M. Neville (called Felbrigg in 1930). The View was occupied by a Mrs E.J. Burstow. The tall grass grew in abundance on wasteground away from the shore. 'Pattie' Loftus (Marie's niece) recalls, 'In the summer we all went about wearing swimsuits. There was no water or sanitation. The grass in summer was over a yard high. My hair was so blonde and bleached that when I was playing in the grass they could not find me!' The lower picture shows the site, Woodward's View, in 1996.

Aerial view of Shoreham Beach, looking north-west, *c.* 1938. The photograph is from an original owned by Mr Fred Witten of Shoreham. Lancing College is the Gothic cathedral-like building top left on the far side of the Adur river. New Shoreham, the old town, is clustered around the church of St Mary's (de Haura). The harbour can be seen in the centre at the top of the photograph. Old Shoreham occupies the top of the picture where new houses can be seen along the Upper Shoreham Road. The bridges, from right to left, are the footbridge, the Norfolk bridge which is of the cantilever type and carries the main coast road to Worthing, the iron railway bridge on the Brighton–Portsmouth line, and the old wooden

toll bridge of 1781, rebuilt 1916, which carried the A27 road westward (now only for pedestrian traffic).
A bypass was built north of the toll bridge. The spit of land known as Shoreham Beach can be seen in the
foreground with Old Fort Road nearest the sea. North of the Old Fort Road is the East Meadway with
Riverside Road beyond. On the north side of Old Fort Road (right) are the bungalows owned by the
comic Will Evans. They were known as the 'pantomime' bungalows as Evans named them after pantos in
which he had starred. Ferry Road crosses the top of East Meadway and Old Fort Road.

King's Drive, looking north-west, 1920s. King's Drive, probably named after King Edward VII, runs south from the main Brighton–Worthing coast road to the Church of the Good Shepherd at the west end of Beach Road. At the junction with the main road there were several shops which along with Ferry Road provided the only shopping on the Beach. This is the only way to the Beach by vehicle, except for the ford from near East Street, which was unsuitable for motor cars, even at very low tide. The motor car in the top photograph is passing a series of lock-up wooden garages. It was very necessary to have a place to keep automobiles under cover near the sea. The salty brine driven by the wind off the sea caused vehicles to rust at a much quicker pace than those inland. The modern photograph shows the realignment of the road seventy-five years on.

King's Drive, looking south-west, 1920s. The Church of the Good Shepherd can be seen at the end of King's Drive where it joins Beach Road. The three shops on the right were originally a tea lodge, a drug store, and a post office. Later the tea lodge was taken over by Reg Leggett as an estate agent's and the drug store became a confectioner's. King's Crescent is by the motor car in the top picture. There are only five dwellings including the shop on the east side of the road, and six on the west not including the three shops. In the lower photograph the road has been realigned to the east and King's Drive ends in a cul-de-sac at its north end. The lower photograph was taken in the car park of the Royal Coach public house and all the shops have disappeared.

Riverside Road, looking east before 1921. The track in the top photograph became Riverside Road. The picture was taken from a position near the track called Weald Dyke. In medieval times the Adur river was called the Weald Ditch, so Weald Dyke could be a relic of this early name. This is the south bank of the Adur, the name of the river from the early seventeenth century. The large houseboat at the end of the track was the *Skylark* and the occupant in 1915 was listed in the directory for that year as a Mr Baguley; to all intents and purposes it was recorded as another bungalow. The *Skylark* appears to be near the site of the south end of the footbridge which was opened in February 1921, the toll at the time being one penny. The railway carriage component of the bungalow on the right can be clearly seen.

Shoreham Beach, the corner of King's Drive and King's Walk, *c*. 1919. Before the Church of the Good Shepherd was built, services were held on the beach and one service by the Bishop of Chichester drew a congregation of some two hundred worshippers. Building work on the church began on 26 April 1913, by Gates of Shoreham, with the foundation stone laid by the Bishop of Lewes. The opening service took place on 16 July 1913 following a procession of the clergy, choir and worshippers. From conception to consecration in little over a year and at a cost of about £750. The Ecclesiastical Parish of Shoreham Beach includes the 'mainland' up to the railway, New Salts Farm Road, and west to The Broadway. The lower photograph shows the building as it is now (1996). It has been altered and enlarged but the outward appearance remains very much the same as in the 1919 view.

Shoreham Beach, looking east, *c*. 1945. The Church of the Good Shepherd stands in isolation. As a young sailor I recall seeing a similar view in September 1945, thousands of miles away from here at a place called Hiroshima, where everything was also flattened except the church (N-B). The army had destroyed much of the original Bungalow Town during the Second World War. The south coast was Hitler's intended invasion target. Jackie Martin came to the Beach in 1947 and recalls, 'It was so bleak that winter and there were no lights, or very few along the Beach, and there were large areas of fields which made getting anywhere after dark a worry for a young girl. On the Beach were concrete slabs and blocks for defence and iron tubes sticking out of the sea. Although the war was over one was reminded of it constantly.'

THE ENTERTAINERS

Old Fort Road, c. 1915. The bungalow, probably Roxburgh, was situated at the east end of Old Fort Road near the Fort and Kingston Bay Road, where at one time or another there was a ferry operating from Kingston near the lighthouse, where the lifeboat station is now. The directory of the time names Mrs S.E. Kerr as the owner or occupier. It must be remembered that at this time there was no television or radio available and any entertainment was self-made. Many, in their spare time from the studio or those just on holiday, took to the sea during the day, and in the evening card games were the usual pursuit. N.E.B. Wolters recalls that some actors and technical staff lost their wages on the evening of pay day. Others, more sensible, took to music for their relaxation. There were usually a few music hall folk who would join in with family parties.

Ferry Road, looking north, 1920s. As its name implies, Ferry Road led to the earlier rowing boat ferry from the hard at the south end of East Street. Ferry Road connects Lower Beach Road and Riverside Road with Beach Road and Old Fort Road to the south. In fact it divides the two latter. The famous Bungalow Stores (extreme right, above) was the major supplier of food and all the requirements of a fairly isolated community. The store was run by the Eade family who had bought it from the founder Mr Pike. The Eades had shops in the High Street, Brunswick Road, and New Road as well as the Ferry Road shop. Part of the shop was a sub-post office and the man behind the grill in those days was Henry Cheal, one of Shoreham's historians, and the author of *Ships and Mariners of Shoreham* (1909) and *The Story of Shoreham* (1921). In 1921 a footbridge replaced the ferries. This is now the main shopping parade for the Beach dwellers.

Ferry Road shops and Flo's Beach Club, *c.* 1920s. This photograph was taken from the newly erected footbridge. Henry Cheal notes that visitors to Bungalow Town referred to Shoreham itself as the 'village'; others, who seem to have a somewhat hazy notion of the geography of the district, refer to Bungalow Town as 'the island'. He also remarks that at high tide the Adur presents the appearance of a fine lake, while at low tide it is reduced to a trickle through a waste of mud, with the attendant smells. Flo's Beach Club was a club and dance hall with various entertainments, the centre of social life on the beach before the Second World War. Florrie Forde was an Australian singer, noted for her singing of such songs as 'Down at the Old Bull and Bush'. She ran the club from a bungalow called Gull's Nest at the east end of Widewater, near the Church of the Good Shepherd (*see* p. 124).

Old Fort Road, *c.* 1915. Pavlova was No. 8 on the south side of Old Fort Road. It was built for Marie Loftus in about 1914. It was Marie (known as the Sarah Bernhardt of the Music Halls) who first introduced people from the stage to Shoreham Beach Bungalow Town. Pavlova, built of wood, was an imposing building with many rooms, each bedroom decorated in a different colour. The large dining room had no fewer than twenty-four heavy oak chairs around the long table. This was decorated with valuable table silver – rose bowls, candelabra, cruets and an epergne. When the house was being finished, her daughter Cecilia (Cissie) was giving impressions of Pavlova and both were enjoying great success. As a tribute Marie named the house Pavlova. The lower 1995 view of the site shows the earlier house has gone, probably blown up at the beginning of the Second World War when the army cleared the Beach, fearing invasion of the south coast.

Shoreham Beach during the First World War. This is a view of the west side of Pavlova. A flagpole/mast has been added to the house. This may have been for the White Ensign or Union Jack, flown during the day. The house became an officers' mess for the pilots of the Royal Flying Corps, and of the Royal Naval Air Service who were training over at the aerodrome just the other side of the Norfolk Bridge. A former salt marsh, the aerodrome was used by flying clubs and aircraft constructors like the Pashley brothers (*see* p. 64).

Marie Loftus was married to Ben Brown, who with Newland and LeClercq formed a minstrel act called 'Black Justice'. The LeClercqs occupied a bungalow called Morningside, 108 Old Fort Road. Cissie Loftus (right), Marie and Ben's daughter, had the bungalow called Cecilia at No. 150 Old Fort Road.

West Beach, 1912. The wreckage is probably the remains of a bungalow called Rattingdean near the Church of the Good Shepherd. It was occupied by Hackenschmidt, the famous wrestler. It is not known if George Hackenschmidt was the owner or tenant as his coach and trainer owned several bungalows west of the church, including Silverstrand, Fairy Dene, Fassifern and Little Fairy Dene. Hackenschmidt can be seen in the top photograph in the right foreground. He would have been around thirty-four at this time. It is recorded that he was carried in and out of the sea by his trainer, Professor Bates, who was a small man, as 'Hack' had tender feet and found it painful to walk on the pebbles!

George Hackenschmidt, 1877–1968. Called the Russian Lion because of his great strength and fearless fighting prowess, he was born in Livonia but later became a naturalized Briton and was managed by his agent, C.B. Cochran the impresario. He first entered the professional wrestling ranks in about 1900, having been amateur European champion in 1898. His two sensational bouts against the Terrible Turk, Armed Madrali, made George a national hero. He retired to London after his fighting days and wrote books. The Australian running coach Percy Cerutty called him 'The greatest living authority on the relationship between mind and body'.

Ernie Mayne made a career as a comic in the late Victorian and Edwardian music halls. He was well known in pantomime in all the northern theatres, playing Jack in *Mother Goose*, and Buttons in *Cinderella* and the clown in many others. Ernie was born in Topsham, Devon (near Exeter) on 17 March 1871. His real name was Percy Ernest Barratt. He once said that he started life as an acrobat, but since he was such a huge figure this statement was probably to produce laughs. He recorded many of his songs for the Gramophone and Typewriter Co. and is known to have made two of the first talking pictures under the direction of Léon Gaumont, who was experimenting as early as 1898 with synchronized phonograph cylinders; in 1900 he demonstrated this at the Paris Exposition. It is not known when Mayne first came to the Beach, but he owned two bungalows and let one to other music hall artists.

HEBE HOTEL,
SHOREHAM-BY-SEA.   *Simply Yours,*
Telephone: SHOREHAM 68.   ERNIE MAYNE.

For many years Ernie owned Simplicity and also Lalerne at 136 Beach Road. We do not know which one he lived in but he often spent a month or so on the Beach when his shows permitted. In 1928 he became the host of a large property in Victoria Road, the Hebe Hotel. He continued to appear at the music halls and Christmas 1928 found him playing the principal comedian in the pantomime *Beauty and the Beast* at London's Lyceum Theatre. This was thought to be his last London appearance and he retired to run his Hebe Hotel. In 1931 he gave up the lease of the Hebe, and moved back to his bungalow Lalerne on the Beach. At Christmas 1936 Ernie came out of retirement to make his last appearance in pantomime, *Robinson Crusoe* at the Connaught Theatre, Worthing. Ernie played Dame Crusoe in the pantomime. The *Worthing Gazette*, 6 January 1937 reported, 'The most popular pantomime ever produced in Worthing'. Ernie Mayne died in the Royal Sussex Hospital on 14 May 1937, aged sixty-six, and he is buried in Shoreham.

Old Fort Road, 1920s. This is 51 Old Fort Road, named Simplicity. The propeller over the doorway may indicate that the bungalow was once owned by an aviator. The man standing in the doorway is thought to be Ernie Mayne who bought the bungalow. Mayne joined with his friend and neighbour, Albert LeFre, who lived next door in Coogee, to buy several bungalows in Beach Road. These dwellings were for letting and were called Hoo-Hoo, Timaru and Silverdale. There were many interesting people living here in the 1920s but the real top-liners of the music hall predominated; indeed no fewer than a dozen of them had been selected to appear in the Royal Command Performance of 1912. Many others appeared in subsequent Royal Performances, several of them more than once. The lower present-day photograph shows the bungalow without the verandah and porch.

Williams,
from Australia,
The Man in the Velvet Suit."

Three notable Australians arrived in this country early in the twentieth century, Albert Whelan, Florrie Forde, and 'Billy' Williams. Billy, whose real name was William Holt Banks, was born in 1877 in the 'outback' among the gold miners and rugged pioneers. He spent his early life working in a racing stable and later became a boundary rider. He liked a bet and was often broke after a failed 'flutter' on the horses. To supplement his income he started to compose and sing comic songs in the rough saloons, taverns, and pubs of the region under the name Billy Williams. Although sturdily built, Billy decided that the outback was a bit too rough for him and in 1901 he came to England with his father to try out his talent on the British public. He was appointed manager of the Marylebone Music Hall, and married an English girl the same year.

Billy Williams was among the first of the Music Hall artists to adopt a personal trade mark. He sported an immaculate blue velvet suit, white spats and, later, a large flowing tie. He always had a fresh flower in his left buttonhole and wore a 'bubbles' hairstyle which made him instantly recognizable to the general public as a great individualist. He was perhaps the first artist to exploit the potential of the new 'phonograph'. He charged £2 10s for each wax cylinder he recorded. This was the first time in history that artists could perform in the living-rooms of the nation. Among the all-time greats of the early part of this century were his 'When Father Papered the Parlour' and 'Willies Wild Woodbines'. He had several bungalows on the Shoreham Beach. He died at the age of thirty-seven and is buried in the Mill Lane cemetery.

Beach Road, looking east, *c.* 1914. Beach Road continues east of Ferry Road as Old Fort Road. Many of the stage people lived on the Beach in bungalows they had built for them. When money was available, they also had extra buildings erected for letting, which gave them a supplementary income. Emu and Kangaroo in the top photograph were owned by Billy Williams, and named as one would expect from someone whose origins lay on the other side of the world. These two bungalows are not recorded in the directory for 1914/15 and the 1930 guide records Lyndhurst but not Emu or Kangaroo. Empty plots are noted so perhaps they caught fire and burned down as did many here, out of reach of the fire brigade. What did survive for posterity was the voice of Billy Williams on wax rolls and gramophone records which even now are played from time to time on the radio. The lower picture shows a scene that would not have been recognized by any of those old Beach dwellers.

EARLY FILM MAKING

The Great Glass Studio, c. 1920. The glass studio was built on a site of about a quarter of an acre to the north-west of the Church of the Good Shepherd on the west beach. There was also a large workshop for the production of stage scenery which was said to be bigger than the studio (it may be the building on the left). There was a twenty-bedroom bungalow nearby which provided accommodation for the actors and cameramen. The studio was some 45 ft by 75 ft and had slightly obscured glass to obviate shadows while filming. It was built in 1915 by the Sealight Film Company formed by F.L. Lyndhurst. Filming could only take place when the light permitted, so for the winter months the place was deserted. Lyndhurst was the producer and when he wanted 'extras' he put a notice on his front gate which read 'People wishing to appear in a film will be allowed to do so free of charge if they present themselves at . . .' such and such a time. Later they could see themselves at the Star Picture House in Church Street.

Presentation to mark one hundred years of cinema, 8 June 1996. Left to right: Louise Brattle (Adur District Council, Leisure), Revd Colin Blagg (Church of the Good Shepherd), Joan Morgan, Frank Gray (Curator, South/East film and video archive).

Joan Morgan unveiled a plaque at the Church of the Good Shepherd on Shoreham Beach to mark Cinema 100. Adur District Council, South-East Arts, and West Sussex County Council combined to organize and fund the event. Joan Morgan (91) was the daughter of Sidney Morgan, a prolific and talented film director who was the major creative force behind the Progress Film Co. After the presentation there was a showing of *A Lowland Cinderella* which starred Joan (then a teenager). This silent film had not been shown for some seventy years and had only recently been discovered in the National Film Archive. It is thought to have been made in 1921 when Joan was 16 and is an hour-long classic melodrama in which she plays Hester Stirling, whose father leaves her penniless.

Lyndora, Arnside, Breezy and Fido, Old Fort Road, *c.* 1915. The golden years on Shoreham Beach were between 1914 and the mid-1920s when, attracted by the quality of light and the pure air of the south coast, the early film makers settled among the sheds and chalets of Bungalow Town and set up studios. Lyndora (left) was the home of Francis Lyndhurst, who built the huge glass studio (*see* p. 117) to make films for his company Sealight. We believe it was Lyndhurst who also founded the Sunny South Film Company. Two early films made in 1914 were *The Jockey* and *The Showman's Dream*, both starring the famous Will Evans.

Between the end of the First World War and the early 1920s about twenty films were made on Shoreham Beach and in parts of the town and airfield; many of them were directed by Sidney Morgan. However, disaster struck in 1922 when the studios were burnt down leaving little that could be used. The effect of the fire and the growth of the film industry in Hollywood led to the decline of Shoreham as a location. The studio buildings were finally removed in the early years of the Second World War to make room for wartime coastal defences.

Francis Lyndhurst was the grandfather of Nicholas Lyndhurst, star of TV shows *Only Fools and Horses* and *Goodnight Sweetheart*. It is comforting to know that Francis's earlier talent has passed down through the generations.

Below, the scene eighty years on.

The Old Fort, 1920s. The Fort is located at the east end of the shingle beach which forms the south bank of the River Adur at this point. It guards the entrance to Shoreham Harbour and is believed to have been started in the Napoleonic era with cannon commanding the coastal area. Said by Wolters to have been one of the 'Palmerston Follies', the fort was not completed until after the end of the Crimean War in 1857. It was still in use for drills and parades until the end of the Victorian period. A photograph of 1896 shows the Sussex Volunteers (about seventy men) drawn up for inspection in full ceremonial uniform. This troop may have been preparing for the Boer War in South Africa. The man in the top photograph is probably Mr Stephen Easter, a local landowner and farmer, who was also the owner of several bungalows. In the photograph below children play on the pebble-silted ruins (1996).

The Old Fort, east of Bungalow Town, 1914. The parade ground of the old fort, now derelict, was used by the newly formed Sunny South Film Company, which made four silent films there. The production in progress (note the cameraman with the manual cine-camera in the lower photograph) is *The Showman's Dream*. A canvas backdrop and set was put up on temporary scaffold and residents and passers-by were invited to be 'extras'. N.E.B. Wolters recalls the making of the film. He says that the script called for a chase after a tiger escapes from a circus fire. The chase went through Old Shoreham, with the 'tiger' (young man in tiger costume) chasing an old woman. Passing the Red Lion Inn at a moment when a none too sober man stepped out of the pub, the 'tiger' turned his attention to the drunk, who turned white and ran off up the Steyning Road. The scene was so funny it was kept in the film.

The Film Studio Gardens, *c*. 1920. Film making on the Beach site was in operation up until the mid-1920s. We have no information on this apparently well laid-out garden. There is nothing in print to show how it was started or constructed, or indeed who commissioned and financed it. In the background one can see the great glass studio building (left) and what appears to be a high fence; it is possible that this doubled as a screen for painted scenery on the other side. Exterior filming was most expensive. Some films like *The Rogues of the Turf* (1922) were shot in England, France and Belgium as well as at the studio in Shoreham. Films were also made on location in Steyning, Beeding and Bramber. *The Mayor of Casterbridge* was partly filmed at the White Horse public house in Steyning and the market scene was set in the High Street of that village. The people on the little bridge do not look like locals; perhaps someone will recognize them as 'stage' personalities. In the lower photograph the building on the extreme left is a children's home in King's Gap.

The Film Studio Gardens. This view (top) is the reverse of the scene on the page opposite. The lead figure of the little boy still exists in private hands. The two staircases were probably used for grand entrances and romantic scenes in the films. Tremendous effort must have gone into making these gardens, because it would not be easy to make flowers and foliage flourish in what must have been a very salt-laden atmosphere on the edge of the English Channel. Stanley Mumford (cameraman) said that Shoreham was the only studio in the country where the artists and key personnel lived on site. They had the time of their lives at this seaside studio, making a regular holiday of it, so much so that when the picture was finished, the director could not get rid of them! Part of the original bank still remains today.

Stanley Dayer-Smith in riding gear. Joan Dayer-Smith recalls, 'My father, Stanley Dayer-Smith was the owner of riding stables in Hendon until a riding accident left him unable to ride. The Dayer-Smiths then came to Shoreham. Their first home was a bungalow in Old Fort Road. Later they moved to a bungalow called Gull's Nest on the west beach just past the Church of the Good Shepherd, next door to the dwelling called Lazyland. In about 1923, when I was ten, three bungalows caught fire. Gull's Nest was one of them.

'It was rebuilt as a two-storey house, the only two-storey brick building on the Beach. It had seven bedrooms. The Dayer-Smiths turned the larger building into a guest house and several well-known jockeys stayed there during Goodwood and Brighton races weeks.

'My father played a stable lad in the 1923 film *Rogues of the Turf*. Some shots were filmed at Easters, Old Salts Farm by the stables. The plot required a racehorse to be stolen in order to miss the race, it was put on a barge opposite King's Gap. Stanley was worried because the horse still had its blanket on and he was afraid that if it went into the water it would get its legs caught and drown. The horse did jump into the water but swam safely to the shore. My older sister and myself had roles in a couple of Shoreham films, although I cannot remember which ones. My mother was taken ill and the family moved to Hove, leasing Gull's Nest to Florrie Forde. It was from this base that she ran 'Flo's' Club on Shoreham Beach.'

Lancing Holiday Camp was at the west end of the Beach conurbation, north of the coast road on farm land near Wenceling Cottages. The photographs were loaned to us by Mary Belton whose parents founded the Holiday Camp business at Nutbourne in 1921 and went on to Lancing in 1922. For the holiday-makers there was the attraction of the seaside, and also the fact that the Shoreham aerodrome was only a field away in those early days of flying. The air races at times always produced a few mishaps to provide interest. Mary Belton, using the 'tips' she got as a young girl, often sneaked away to the airfield and had trips in one of the old biplanes at 5s a flight. This was in the days of Alan Cobham's 'flying circus'.

BIBLIOGRAPHY

Adur Leisure, Adur District Council. *Film Making on Shoreham Beach 1914–1923*, 1995.

Blagg, Revd Colin. *Church of the Good Shepherd, Shoreham Beach, 1913–1988*, 1988

Bull, D. & Oliver, L.K. *Shoreham Memories*, Shoreham, Nostalgia Publications, 1980.

Camden, W. *Magna Britannia*, Amsterdam, Guilielmum Blaeu, 1639.

Cartwright, E. *Western Division of Sussex, Rape of Bramber*, J.B. Nichols, 1830.

Cheal, H. *The Ships and Mariners of Shoreham*, F.M. Blake, 1909.

— *The Story of Shoreham*, Hove, Combridges, 1921.

Colquhoun, E. & Nethercoate-Bryant, K. *Around Old and New Shoreham*, Hove, Goldleaf, 1989.

Cooper, W. *Smuggling in Sussex*, Newcastle-on-Tyne, F. Graham 1966 (reprint of 1858).

Dallas-Brett, R. *The History of British Aviation, 1908–1914*, John Hamilton, 1933.

Davis, N. *The Saints Before*, Worthing, Gadds, 1990.

Farrant, J.H. *The Rise and Decline of a South Coast Sea Faring Town; Brighton 1550–1750*, University of Sussex, occasional paper.

Hill, R. *Old Shoreham Villages and Farms*, Vol. I, 1995 & Vol. II, 1996. Shoreham, published by author.

Horsefield, T.W. *History of Sussex*, 2 Vols, Lewes, 1835.

Kelly's Sussex Directories for 1903, 1906 and 1915.

Kerridge, R.G.P. *History of Lancing*, Chichester, Philimore, 1978.

Martin, E.G. 'Shoreham and its Struggle with the Adur', *Sussex County Magazine*, March 1930.

Norman, M. *A Walkabout Guide to Shoreham*, Shoreham, Marlipins Museum, 1984.

Salmon, E.F. & Pilmore, A. *The Two Shorehams by Two Inhabitants*, Hove, Emery & Son, 1902.

Brandon, P. (ed.) *New Shoreham Census Returns 1881*, Shoreham & Southwick History Workshop, 1986.

Sussex Archaeological Collections, Lewes 1848–present.

Sussex Notes & Queries, Lewes, SAS.

Victoria County History of Sussex, Vols II and VI, Leicester University Press.

White, Revd J. *Southlands, Workhouse and Hospital*, Hospital League of Friends, 1990.

Wolters, N.E.B. *Bungalow Town, Theatre and Film Colony*, Shoreham, 1985.

Wynne, C. *The Story of Shoreham Grammar School*, Old Shorehamers' Association, 1977.

A beach buggy!

BRITAIN IN OLD PHOTOGRAPHS